# how to
# COUPON
## *effectively*

# LAUREN GREUTMAN
### iamthatlady.com

# ABOUT THE AUTHOR

**Lauren Greutman** is the frugal living expert behind the popular money saving blog *iamthatlady.com*. At the age of 25, she and her husband Mark were in over $40,000 worth of debt and were running a deficit of $1,000 per month. They knew they needed to change so they put together a budget. After realizing they were spending $1,000 per month on food, they decided cutting back was a necessity in order to save money.

Lauren turned to couponing and meal planning and was able to get that $1,000 per month grocery budget down to $200 per month. She fed her family on $200 per month for three years, while becoming debt free.

She started her blog after teaching years of coupon seminars, and has a passion for changing the way busy moms view couponing. She sees her website as a tool to reach more people with her message that couponing doesn't have to take a lot of time, if you do it correctly.

Lauren married her husband Mark in 2002, and they have four young children. She resides in Upstate NY where she still teaches coupon seminars and runs her blog with Mark, all while chasing after her children and drinking enormous amounts of coffee.

# NOTE FROM THE AUTHOR

**Couponing is an important part of how we save money** and still enjoy life while staying within our budget. I know that getting started with couponing can seem like a daunting task, so that's why I decided to write this book. I wanted to write a simple, easy to understand book that anyone can read, so you can quickly start saving money and begin to see the financial benefits of couponing. I believe that anyone can save a significant amount of money with coupons as long as they follow some simple rules and know the basics.

Almost everyone who starts couponing does so with the goal to save money, but many don't know where to start or how to do it effectively. Couponing is a learned skill, and it takes time to master it. It takes practice to establish an effective routine that works for you and your family. I remember years ago when I first started using coupons, I was completely overwhelmed. I didn't know anything about where to get coupons or how to save with them. I was completely lost and I almost gave up. But then I started picking up little tricks and tips to help me save more money and time. I learned a lot over the years, and I want to share with you some of the most basic, yet most important things that have helped me save a lot of money and be a successful couponer.

I guarantee that in just two hours per week I can teach you how to save 50% off your grocery bill. This adds up over time and can save you thousands of dollars per year!

In this book, I will start from the basics and will walk you through, step by step, and show you how to save the most every week in the grocery store. One common misconception about couponing is that you have to have a lot of free time in order to save a lot of money. This simply isn't true. You decide how much time you want to devote to it. You can spend 45 minutes per week or 10 hours per week – it's all about developing a system that works around your schedule. In this book, I aim to teach you how to do this in two hours or less and I know that by following my simple tips you will see success no matter how much time to put into it.

I hope you enjoy this book because I enjoyed writing it for you. Thanks so much for taking the time to read it!

*Lauren Greutman*

If at any time you are reading this book and have a question, please feel free to reach out to me! It's best reach to reach me at *lauren@iamthatlady.com*, my Facebook page [*facebook.com/iamthatlady*], or on Twitter [*@iamthatlady*].

I want to help you any way I can, so just let me know what questions you have!

# TABLE OF CONTENTS

# 1

## WHY COUPON?

**If your boss came to you today** and offered you an extra $25 per hour to sit at a table and clip out paper squares, would you do it? What if your boss then told you that if you worked efficiently and planned, you could make up to $50.00 per hour? That's how I see couponing. It is virtually a pay raise, for simply planning and clipping paper. With just a few simple strategies you can see HUGE savings. My goal is to save 50% off my grocery bill each week. That means if I spend $75.00, I aim to save $75.00 between coupons and store sales. If I just spent two hours planning and executing that trip, that works out to $32.50 per hour. Not too shabby, huh?

**Thinking of couponing as an hourly wage does one important thing: It keeps you from spending too much time on it.**

We all know that you can spend 20 hours per week and drive around to 5 different stores, but if you are only saving 40% and then spending more in gas money, what are you truly saving? Saving $70 when you spend 20 hours is an hourly wage of $3.50 per hour; no one would work for that. My goal is to help you save the same amount of money but in more than half the time!

Let's face it—we are all busy moms constantly running around. We drive to and from baseball practice and dance classes, help kids with homework, cook dinners, pack lunches, all while possibly working outside the home and trying to keep the house at least somewhat "clean." We are already running on empty, and the thought of adding one more thing to your ever growing 'to do' list is daunting. BUT if your boss offered you $50.00 per hour, would you take it? Would you make the time? My guess is that you probably would, so think of using coupons the same way; just a few hours each week can significantly contribute to your household finances.

# 2

## COUPON LINGO

**When you first start using coupons,** you may feel as if everyone else is speaking 'Couponese.' BOGO, ECB, MIR, what do all of these acronyms mean?

In this chapter I break down the Coupon Lingo to help you start talking like a pro! You may want to print this page and keep it with your coupon collection for easy reference.

|  |  |
| --- | --- |
| $1/2 | $1 off of 2 products |
| B1G1 or BOGO | Buy one, get one free |
| 5/23 Smart Source | This coupon came from the May 23rd newspaper |
| SS | Smart Source coupon insert |
| RP | Red Plum coupon insert |
| P&G | Proctor and Gamble coupon insert |
| GM | General Mills coupons insert |
| Peelie | A coupon stuck to the front of a product |
| IP | Internet printable coupon |
| Mfr | Manufacturer coupon |
| ECB's | Extra Bucks, valid only at CVS |
| SCR's | Single Check Rebates, valid only at Rite Aid |

## COUPON ABBREVIATIONS

|  |  |
|---|---|
| WYB | When you buy |
| OOP | Out of pocket |
| FAR | Free after rebate |
| MIR | Mail in rebate |
| +UP | Rite Aid's reward program, similar to ECB's program at CVS |
| OYNO | $$ off your next order [Catalina] |
| YMMV | Your Mileage May Vary—You may be able to get this deal at one store, but not another |
| CPN | Coupon |
| DND | Do Not Double—Will be on a coupon that is not intended to double |
| Filler | An item or items you buy in order to get your total up to a certain amount in order to use a percentage off coupon |
| Stacking | Using a manufacturer's coupon in addition to a store coupon |
| ETS | Excludes trial size |

Now that you understand coupon language,
you are ready to start looking for them.

# 3

## WHERE TO FIND COUPONS

**Finding coupons can be easy** if you know where to look. In my opinion, the best place to find coupons is online; there are SO many great resources available to you for free. I still get my Sunday newspaper and love those coupons, but free coupons are even better! In this chapter I want to give you an idea of where to start looking for the best coupons out there. They are not all for processed foods like you may think; there are actually tons of coupons for healthy products, you just have to know where to look for them.

Before we begin, I want to encourage you to set up a separate email account just for couponing. You'll be signing up for a lot of things, and I would hate for your personal email box to get filled with unnecessary junk mail.

Here is an overview of where you can find coupons:

- Sunday newspaper

- Free samples

- Magazines

- Your mailbox (Bricks coupons)

- Printable coupon websites [*bit.ly/coupon-database-10*]

- Peelie coupons

- Blinkie coupons

- Hangtag coupons

- Email newsletters

- Facebook

- Company websites

- Emailing companies

Now I am going to break down these sections and tell you exactly how to get coupons from each!

## SUNDAY NEWSPAPER

A great place to find coupons is your Sunday newspaper. Each Sunday the number of coupon inserts will vary. One that comes in the Sunday paper is Smartsource. When I am writing the coupon matchups for my blog, you will see the date of the newspaper that the insert came in, followed by SS for Smartsource (Example 3/1 SS). Most coupon websites you visit will use the same type of abbreviations. (If you decide to keep the coupon insert whole, without cutting the coupons, write the date at the top of the front page and you will know where to cut your coupons from when I do a match up.)

You will also find coupon inserts from Red Plum (RP is the abbreviation). Smartsource and RedPlum

 coupon inserts are included in most Sunday newspapers. Some weeks we may get one insert from each company in the

paper, sometimes we get lucky and there are two or maybe even three from each.

A few times a year you will receive inserts from companies such as General Mills and P&G; these inserts have coupons for their own products. My general rule of thumb is to buy one paper for every two members of my household. Often, I might get more than that if there is a crazy sale or coupon, but I usually stick with the three papers that get delivered to my house (since we have six people in our family). If you have friends, neighbors or family members that don't coupon themselves, ask them if they would save their coupon inserts for you if cannot afford to buy papers, but the $2.00 I pay every week for each paper is well worth the investment.

## COUPON INSERT KEY

### Coupon Insert Abbreviation Key

Smart Source = SS

Red Plum = RP

Proctor & Gamble = P&G

General Mills = GM

## PRINTABLE COUPON WEBSITES

Coupons that are found online and printed at home are called printable coupons. You can print these coupons for free from these websites:

- coupons.com

- smartsource.com

- redplum.com

If you are going to be printing a lot of coupons, I recommend getting yourself a good printer. I personally recommend a Brother Laser Printer, you can find one on sale for around $60.00 and you won't pay for toner for months! If you plan on printing coupons from your phone or iPad, you will need a HP Photosmart printer.

## FACEBOOK

To find coupons on Facebook, make sure that you 'Like' your favorite product pages. Product pages frequently have coupons for their products and even FREE coupon giveaways! The catch with the free coupon giveaways it that they disappear quickly, so if you see one, jump on it right away or else it may be gone.

## COMPANY WEBSITES

If you are looking to save on a specific brand's product, head over to their website. Often, they have printable coupons available to print for free directly from there.

## MAGAZINES

Subscribing to magazines is a great way to get coupons! Two of my favorites are All You and Weight Watchers. All You is full of coupons, and also has great money saving articles, recipes, and frugal living tips. You can find a subscription deal for All You on my site monthly. Weight Watchers includes some healthier coupons for things like cheese, vegetables, and more. Don't pay full price for either of these because on *iamthatlady.com*, we usually find deals for over 50% off the retail price.

## FREE SAMPLES

Samples are another great way to get coupons. Often free samples arrive in the mail along with coupons for that product. I received a Kashi sample once and it came with a high value $3 off coupon, which is not your typical coupon value.

**Bonus tip\* Check out the free sample carts when grocery shopping, they frequently give away high value coupons for the products they are handing out as samples.**

# EMAIL COMPANIES DIRECTLY

One of my favorite ways to get coupons is to email companies whose products I really like. I tell them that I love their product and share a personal story about why it's better than the rest. Remember that a real person is reading your email, so you need to be genuine in your compliment. Most of the time they will send you free coupons in the mail.

These are companies you should consider contacting:

| | |
|---|---|
| Bolthouse Farms | Coffee-mate creamer |
| Amy's Organic Foods | Organic Valley |
| Glutino (gluten free) | Stonyfield Farms |
| Driscoll's Berries | Mott's |
| Birdseye | Starkist |
| Tropicana | Luna Bars |
| Lean Cuisine | Uncle Ben's |

Blue Diamond                    Wholly Guacamole

Tide                            Pepperidge Farm

Blue Bunny                      Udi's (gluten free)

Ore Ida                         Alexia

I would recommend writing something like this:

> Hello {Company},
>
> My name is Lauren and I'm writing to let you know I really love your products! I'm always telling my friends and family how well {product name} works; it even gets the stubborn grass stains out of my son's white baseball pants. Thank you for making my job as a mom easier. {product name} is simply the best and I'm so grateful!
>
> Sincerely,
>
> *Lauren*

## PEELIE, BLINKIE, AND HANGTAG COUPONS

When you are walking around the grocery store, you will often find peelie coupons. These are coupons that are stuck to the package and can be peeled off to use at the register. The coupon is intended to be used only on the item you are purchasing—not to be removed from the product and used at another store.

Another coupon you may find while walking around the grocery store is called a blinkie coupon. These come from the little blinking machines in the aisles of your grocery store. They are usually right in front of the product that the coupon is for. My advice is to grab them and hold on to them. Instead of using them as soon as you get them (unless the product is on sale that day), it makes more sense to wait until that product is on sale another day.

A hangtag coupon is usually hung around the product on the shelf. Similar to a peelie coupon, this one is intended to be used only on the item you are purchasing.

## EMAIL NEWSLETTERS

Make sure you sign up for your favorite companies' email newsletters. They frequently send out coupon offers via email with links that are only for you to use. Remember to set up that separate email account – you will thank me later.

# 4

## DIGITAL COUPONS

**The use of digital offers is rising,** so why not take advantage of it to save yourself some money?

In this chapter, I will share my favorite money saving apps and how to use them. There are a few that do not require use of a mobile device, so don't let that hold you back from digital coupons.

## FAVADO

Favado is an app that provides the weekly store sales of most grocery stores in the US and matches them with available coupons. The app also includes unadvertised sales that were not listed in the weekly flyer—so you can take your favorite coupon

matchups on the go! *[bit.ly/ favadoapp10]*

In addition, you can compare products from a few different stores to find the best price on an item. If you need bread, you can quickly find the best price in town and go to that store, instead of looking through half a dozen flyers.

## SAVINGSTAR

SavingStar can be used on either your computer or your smartphone. After setting up an account, you simply register your grocery store loyalty cards in SavingStar, accept 'your offers,' and save money. The money does not come out of your total at the register; instead, when you redeem one of their offers, the money is deposited into your digital SavingStar account. When you reach $5.00,

you can withdraw that money from Paypal, get a bank deposit, or even an Amazon gift card.

Above you can see some of the new offers I had in my account. You simply click 'I want this' and once you purchase the product with your store loyalty card the money is automatically deposited in your SavingStar account.

There has been some confusion concerning whether you can use manufacturer coupons along with SavingStar offers. As of this writing, the official response is that "they were not intended to be used together." However, there are instances when you are permitted to use SavingStar offers with manufacturer coupons. For any SavingStar offer that is for multiple products, there is no restriction on manufacturer coupon use. For example, if there is a SavingStar offer to save $5 when you spend $18 on any OFF! products, then you would be able to use manufacturer coupons on these products in the same transaction.

## IBOTTA

Ibotta is a simple app. You view your offers before you go shopping, then take a picture of your receipt after you have purchased those offers. Afterwards, cash is deposited into your Paypal account! Very simple and easy! Some stores offer immediate redemption, meaning that you don't even have to scan your receipt, and the money is still deposited into your account.

You can see in the picture above a few of the offers available at Target. If I were to purchase the Special K protein bars, I would scan a picture of my receipt or get immediate redemption, and get $0.75 into my Ibotta account. You can also use manufacturer coupons along with an Ibotta reward. Your store has to be a participating store in order to use Ibotta. You can find a list of those stores here: *bit.ly/ibotta10*

## CHECKOUT 51

Checkout 51 is similar to Ibotta, but it works at ANY store with ANY receipt. I love this because I can

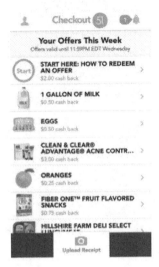

buy something at Aldi and use Checkout 51 to save even more money!

They have some of my favorite offers for things like milk, eggs, and fruit. It works the same way that Ibotta does—buy the product, scan the receipt, and get money in your account. *[bit.ly/checkout51-10]*

## STORE DIGITAL COUPONS

Your store may have an app or digital coupons. Go to their website or search the app store to see if they have their own digital savings system. Most of them do these days!

## TARGET'S CARTWHEEL APP

Target has its own app called the Cartwheel App. It takes a percentage off of certain products right at the register.

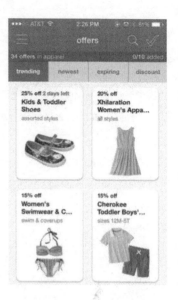

The best part about it is that you can combine Cartwheel offers with Target Store coupons and manufacturer coupons. You can also get money back using Ibotta and Checkout51 too!

Using digital coupons is like icing on the cake for me. I save in the store using paper coupons, and then get money back by using SavingStar, Ibotta, and Checkout51.

26

# 5

## WHAT ARE
## CATALINA COUPONS?

**One type of coupon that** you can only find inside the store is called a Catalina coupon. These print out of a Catalina coupon printer that sits next to the cash register.

They get their name from the company that manages these coupons—Catalina Marketing. They target your purchases and are personalized based on your past, current and expected future buying behaviors.

There are three types of Catalina coupons:

1. Manufacturer Catalinas

2. OYNO Catalinas

3. Store Catalinas

You will need to check that the light on top of the Catalina printer is green so that you know it is working. If the light is red or it is not on at all, the machine is broken or off and will not print any Catalina coupons for you.

## MANUFACTURER CATALINAS

If you get a Catalina that is a manufacturer coupon, it cannot be stacked with another manufacturer coupon. These Catalinas are printed on paper with the store logo it was printed from. Keep in mind that many stores will not accept a Catalina with another store's logo on it.

These manufacturer Catalinas are a form of advertising that a company purchases; they're often triggered to print when a competitor's product is purchased. For example: Coffee-mate will purchase a Catalina coupon to print when someone buys

International Delight Coffee cream. These coupons also print based on your purchase history. I've always gotten baby food coupons when I've purchased baby food; likewise, I get gluten free Catalinas because I eat gluten-free.

## OYNO CATALINAS

If you get a Catalina that is a $$ off coupon, you can use it on your next order (OYNO) on any item in the store. Think of this Catalina as cash towards your next order total. This Catalina can be used with other store and manufacturer coupons you have. If you have an OYNO Catalina and you use it to pay for an item that triggers another Catalina to print, this is called 'rolling' your Catalinas.

## STORE CATALINAS

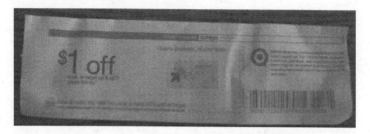

Every once in a while, a Catalina will print out as a store coupon. I have seen these a lot at Target. These can be stacked with a manufacturer coupon to help save you more. All you have to do is remember the three types of Catalinas and you will be in tip-top shape.

# 6

## HOW TO AVOID THE #1 MISTAKE NEW COUPONERS MAKE

**Did you know it's possible to coupon** and spend more money? It is, and I've heard from many people that have couponed themselves into more debt because they haven't paid attention to a few key things. The biggest mistake people make when using coupons is using them right away. This is also the best way to fail at couponing. Why? Because you need to wait for the item to go on sale before you use the coupon. There is one exception to this; when you find a coupon for something that you frequently use and you were going to buy it anyway.

You will see that sales and coupons don't always come out on the same week, so hold on to the coupon until you see that sale. Don't worry about your coupons expiring; don't rush out on the last day of the month to use all of your coupons because mostly likely the same ones will come out next month.

By waiting to use those coupons, you turn a good sale price into a great sale price, therefore leaving more money in your pocket for other things. When you begin couponing and don't yet know the ins and outs, it's quite simple (and costly!) to make this mistake. If you use coupons on items that are not on sale, you'll end up spending a lot more money than you should. You won't be happy with the results and you will be left wondering how it's possible to start using coupons and actually save money. But once you are aware of this pitfall, you know how to avoid it. Remember, keep your coupon until the item is on sale and then use it!

Another way to fail at couponing is getting every deal that you see. If you don't need it, then don't buy it unless you can donate it. When I first started couponing, I ran around to get every deal I could find. I realized I was spending more time organizing all these deals and running from store to store, instead of spending time on the things that I needed most (like food). After all, you can't feed your family dental cleanser, toothpaste, and laundry detergent!

# 7

# HOW TO READ COUPONS

**The fine print on coupons confused me** when I first started using them. You need to make sure that you are reading the fine print, because it will help you at the register.

Here are some basic rules for how to read a coupon:

1.  You can use 1 coupon per item. If you want 10 boxes of pasta, you need 10 coupons. If you have a $1 off of 2 coupon, you will get $1 off of both, not $1 off of each. For example: If you have a box of pasta priced at $1.00 and you bought 2 and used a $1.00 off 2 coupon, you would pay $0.50 per box. You cannot use a $1 off of 2 items and $1 off of 1 of the same item together.

2.  Two words people often confuse are transaction and purchase. Transaction means the items scans and you pay. Purchase means per product. In the Gain coupon above, the coupon says '1 coupon per purchase.' this means if you have more than one of the same coupon you can use it in the same transaction. P&G coupons are also known for saying "Limit 4 like coupons per transaction or shopping trip." This means that you can use four of the same coupon per transaction. It does not mean 4 total P&G coupons per transaction; you can have 4 coupons for Scope mouthwash and 4 deodorant coupons you can use all 8 in 1 transaction.

3.  Check for size exclusions. If there are no size exclusions I try to use it on the smallest item I can find, that way I can get it for free or close to free! This might run contrary

to common wisdom which holds that the larger size you purchase, the best 'per unit' price you will pay. But when a coupon with a fixed dollar savings is part of the equation, it usually becomes the smallest size package that has the best 'per unit' price. You can see the coupon above does not have a size exclusion, if you can find a travel sized Gain priced at $1.00 you would be able to get it for free!

Hopefully this information helps clear up some misconceptions about what the fine print on coupons actually mean. We always want to make sure we are couponing the right way and using our coupons correctly and ethically on the products they are meant for. Do NOT use a coupon on an item that it is not intended for. By reading the fine print you will also avoid any embarrassment at the cash register!

# 8

# HOW TO ORGANIZE
# YOUR COUPONS

**Once you have started your collection of coupons,** it is so important to keep them organized. There are many different ways to do this, and the way you choose is up to you. There is no right or wrong way to organize (except maybe in the bottom of your purse.) What works for you is what is going to help you save the most amount of money.

Here are four popular methods for coupon organization:

## ACCORDION METHOD

A simple and inexpensive accordion style folder is used for this method. You can get a larger one at stores like Walmart for about $5 or a smaller ones at a Dollar Store for $1.00.

- **Pros: Really quick to clip and file. Spend little time organizing them. Easily file random coupons lying around your house.**

- **Cons: You may have to flip through the coupons a little more with this type of method. Can be messy and hard to find coupons.**

I would recommend this method for the "casual couponer." This person clips coupons only for items that they know they are going to use. The casual couponer usually only gets one paper, clips it, and carries her coupons along in her purse.

## WHOLE INSERT METHOD

Another method that many couponers use is called the Whole Insert Method. Using this method, you would keep the coupon insert whole and write the date on the top. When you need to find a specific coupon from a match-up on my site, simply look at the corresponding date and code (SS, RP, etc.) The major advantage of this method is that you won't be cutting coupons that you don't need which will save time. The downside is that you may forget about some of the coupons that you do have in the insert because you didn't actually cut them out. I am a very hands-on person and I found that cutting the coupons works best for me. Once again, trial and error will help you decide which you feel more comfortable with.

## COUPON BINDER METHOD

The method of organizing that I prefer to use is the Coupon Binder Method. This is a large binder organized

with baseball card holders [*bit.ly/couponbinder10*]. All of the cut coupons are organized by categories so that I can find a specific coupon within seconds. I know exactly where to look and how many of each coupon I have because multiples are kept in the same pocket.

## When I used a coupon binder my categories were:

- **Bread/Beverages/Breakfast**
- **Dairy/Meat**
- **Household**
- **Health and Beauty**
- **Canned/Boxed items**
- **Frozen**
- **Snack Foods**

Your categories may differ a bit, but at least this is a starting point for organizing your binder. If you would like to watch a video about how I organize my binder, you can watch that here: [*bit.ly/couponbinder10*]

There really is no right or wrong method to organizing your coupons. You just have to figure out what works best for you. I used a binder for two years and now I am back to an accordion file based on preference.

Organizing your coupons is such an important thing. Have you heard that one hour of planning will save you four hours of execution down the road? If you are at the store with a purse full of coupons, and you keep dropping them and can't find anything, then you are not going to save as much money as someone who has a binder or an accordion file and is well organized. Think about what works best for you. Where do you want to save yourself the most amount of time—at home or in the grocery store? Finding the method that works for you will save you time and money in the long run.

# 9

## KNOW YOUR STORE'S COUPON POLICY

**Now that you have your coupons organized** and understand how to read them, the next thing to do is to get to know your stores' coupon policies. You can usually find them on their website or at the customer service desk in the store. My grocery store has them laminated and displayed in the store and you can request a photocopy for yourself.

If you don't know your store's coupon policy, it can be stressful to plan your shopping trips, and you may miss out on deals. I recommend making a copy of their coupon policy to keep with your coupons at all times. If there is a problem with a transaction or an employee isn't familiar with the coupon policy, you can pull out your copy to show them.

When you first start couponing it is extremely important that you do your research. When you know the rules, your grocery trips will be faster, easier and you will spend less money. So remember, before you go into a Rite Aid, Walgreen's, CVS, etc. you should know everything about their coupon policies and have a copy in your binder or accordion file.

Earlier I told you that the main reason people quit couponing is because they end up spending more than saving, and that's what the stores and manufacturers want you to do! But we are smarter than that and we will continue to cut and organize our coupons and be very strategic about using them. If you're missing out on deals you don't know about because you don't know the correct store policy, you will be missing out on saving more money.

50

# 10

## BUDGETING AND SETTING YOURSELF UP FOR SUCCESS

**It's time to start putting everything together.** You have your coupon collection, you are organized, you know the store policies, and you are ready to save! Now we are going to talk a little bit about budgeting.

Do you have to keep your budget low and learn how to feed your family on a limited amount of money? My husband and I have decided to only use cash for groceries, so every two weeks, we take out our grocery money. This amount varies from $100 to $150 per week, depending on what our schedule looks like. The number one reason that we use cash is so that we do not go over our budget. If you use a debit card, it's very easy to go over a few dollars each time you are at the store, and before you know it you're at the end of the month and you've gone over your budget for the month by $50. Instead of using a debit card, we keep a little envelope that is marked "groceries" and the cash we put in it every two weeks is what we use.

When deciding on a budget, I have heard others say they allot $15 to $20 per person per week, but every family is different. We decided on $100—$150 per week; you may elect to spend $200 a week. I want you to focus on a realistic goal for your family when you are figuring out what your budget will be. Because if you don't stick to it, you may end up spending more money than you would have if you hadn't started couponing.

A great way to start your budget is to figure out the average you have been spending on groceries for the past three months. If you haven't been using cash, you will need to obtain your debit or credit card statements and add up all your grocery charges, then divide that by the number of weeks you included. Use that number as your budget for the first month. Sticking to it is the first step, decreasing it is next. To check out a cool budgeting program, go to *bit.ly/mlg-tools*.

Once you've maintained your budget for a month, I recommend challenging yourself to start the 1/3—1/3—1/3 budgeting system.

## Set Up 1/3, 1/3, 1/3 Budget

1/3 of your budget spent on fresh produce, dairy, meat

1/3 of your budget spent on items you need for the week

1/3 of your budget spent on loss leaders and stock up deals

This means that 1/3 of the budget is for fresh produce, meats and dairy items; 1/3 of the budget is for other items that you need for the week like cereal, pasta, peanut butter etc., and 1/3 of the budget is goes towards 'loss leaders' (more on this in Chapter 14) and stock up sales to help you gradually build a small stockpile. Once you do this for six weeks (the end of one sale cycle), you should have a pretty decent stockpile to help cut that grocery budget down significantly every week.

Here is where knowing when to use your coupons and when to hold onto them is important when sticking to a budget. Assume that you have a $75 weekly budget for groceries and you have a $1 off 3 Pop Tart coupon. The Pop Tarts are not on sale and are $3 a box. If you buy them now and use your coupon, you will get 3 boxes for $2.66 each, and you just spent 11% of your weekly food budget on Pop Tarts. Does that make sense? Do you really need them? These are all questions that you wouldn't have asked yourself without having a weekly budget. Studies show that you also make healthier food choices when you have a set grocery budget; it forces you to choose between Pop Tarts and apples.

Now let's assume that you are spending $200 a week on groceries. I challenge you to lower that by 10% to 20% and then start using your coupons. Over time, try to lower that amount by another 10%. It took me about 3 months to find the right budget for us. Most people who try to slash their budget drastically realize they can't stick to it, and end up going over. The point of a budget is to stay under it, so you need a realistic amount. If you are continuously going over, it is because your budget is too low. Try raising it a bit for a couple weeks and see if that works better for you.

The grocery store matchups on *iamthatlady. com* are for my local grocery stores, and I also do match ups for Rite Aid, Target, CVS, and Walgreens [*bit.ly/iatl-matchups*]. You'll want to find someone that does matchups for your local stores, so go to *iamthatlady.com* and search for "National Blogger Page" to find bloggers in your state that do matchups for your local stores.

56

# 11

## UNDERSTANDING SALE CYCLES

**Knowing the sale cycles is very helpful** when navigating the coupon world. Coupons and store sales usually run in a 6 to 8 week cycle. There are two types of sale cycles—seasonal and yearly. Seasonal sale cycles usually rotate around the seasons. For example: January is National Oatmeal Month, so that's you will see a lot of oatmeal coupons and sale prices on oatmeal. In February, it will be chocolate because of Valentine's Day. You want to keep track of when certain coupons come out so you can figure out what month to stock up on that item. Yearly cycles are rotating sales that happen all year long.

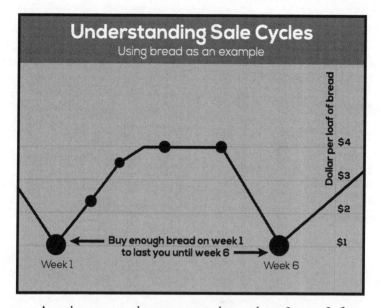

**Understanding Sale Cycles**
Using bread as an example

Dollar per loaf of bread

$4

$3

$2

$1

Buy enough bread on week 1
to last you until week 6

Week 1

Week 6

Another example: my store has a buy 1 get 2 free bread sale that happens every 6-8 weeks. Because I pay attention, I know that I need to buy 9 loaves of bread to get us through to the next sale cycle. By shopping the sale cycle on that 1 item I am saving over $100 a year! Imagine doing that on 10 items, you could save up to $1,000 per year without even picking up a coupon!

Remember that you want to keep your coupons until that item goes on sale, unless it's something that you are running out of or really need. By doing it this way, you will keep your costs the lowest. I can't say this enough: ***the main reason people quit using coupons is because they end up spending more money than they are saving.*** The reason this happens is because they will get a coupon for something and use it right away. But that's not the way we play the game! That's the way the manufacturers want you to play the game but you aren't going fall for that.

# 12

## MEAL PLANNING USING COUPONS

**Once your budget is set,** use your grocery store ads, coupons, and what you already have in your pantry and to begin meal planning. First, look for sales that you can stack your coupons with and create a 'Free or Cheap" list of these deals for the week. Then start creating your menu around those items and the meat that is on sale.

> **\*BONUS HINT\*** Find out when your store discounts its meats; it's usually when the meats are nearing their expiration dates. My store discounts them every morning. Meat is good for three months as long it's frozen right after your purchase.

I'm going to share with you a weekly shopping trip process and menu that I put together for $75.00:

# THE WEEKLY 'FREE AND CHEAP' LIST

1. I found an Asian orange stir-fry mix for only $0.75 cents, so I will make a meal with that as the base.

2. I got a great deal on cream cheese and immediately decided to make homemade Alfredo Sauce.

3. There was a sale and coupon for spaghetti and I got it for $0.50 per box. That will go nicely with the Alfredo Sauce.

4. I had a coupon for Mission Tortillas and they were on sale, so I will use those to make quesadillas and chicken fajitas.

5. I found a deal on black beans. We always have them in our pantry, they are high in protein and they can be used in so many different meals. I will make black beans and rice.

6. Chicken was the meat on sale this week, so I bought two large packages. That should last us two weeks.

## OTHER SALE ITEMS

1. I got a really great price on a large bag of fish sticks, which are not the healthiest option, but come in handy every once in a while when we need a quick and easy meal. So, one dinner this week will be fish sticks and

homemade French fries because they were cheap and I can just throw them in the freezer until I need them. I already had the potatoes at home.

2.  I bought green peppers and onions to make chicken fajitas. I pre-cut and froze them in a Ziploc bag until I am ready to use them. I used the chicken that I purchased on sale, and the Mission tortillas that were on my Free or Cheap list.

3.  I found cheese on sale to use for the chicken fajitas and quesadillas.

4.  Pizza dough and mozzarella cheese were both on sale, so I picked up some of those for pizza. I already had a small can of tomato sauce.

5.  Fish tacos – used corn tortillas I had at home with leftover fish sticks.

6.  I found a marked down pork loin. I will throw that in the freezer until it is time to eat it.

## CURRENT PANTRY ITEMS

1.  We had ground beef in our freezer so I used that to make the Cincinatti chili.

2.  I also had the crushed tomatoes and rice in my pantry.

# MY DINNER MENU FOR THE WEEK

- **Homemade Cincinnati chili over pasta.**

- **Homemade pizza and salad**

- **Fish tacos**

- **Chicken fajitas, rice, and green beans**

- **Orange Chicken (with Asian stir fry mix), peas, rice**

- **Chicken Parmesan with salad**

- **Pasta and homemade Alfredo sauce with broccoli**

- **Quesadillas w/ veggie**

- **Pork loin w/ mashed potatoes and veggies**

It cost me under $75 for all of the ingredients that I got on my grocery trip which is 1 and 1/2 weeks of meals for my family. That is less than $10 per meal for all of us. Your amounts will vary based on family size, eating habits and the available deals for that week.

I just wanted to give you an idea of how I start my meal planning, grocery shopping and couponing to maximize my savings. Make sure you plan your meals out and always bring your coupons to the store with you. With this meal planning method, I have already planned out 1-2 weeks of food, so I will only need to stop at the grocery store a couple times to pick up things like dairy and fresh produce towards the middle of the second week.

Start by trying my method to figure out how to start your meal planning and actually make couponing work for you. Remember, you want coupons to save you money. You want to get things for the lowest price and not use a coupon just because you have it.

## FREE MEAL PLANNING WORKBOOK

To get my FREE Meal planning workbook, you can sign up for my daily email list where I send you an update once a day on all of the money saving tips, recipes, and frugal living articles I've written for the day. This workbook comes complete with printable shopping lists and menus for you to use to help plan your grocery trip. [*bit.ly/meal-planning-workbook*]

## ALDI MEAL PLANS

If you aren't quite sure how this is going to work for you—trust me it can

There is always another option though. That option is Aldi.

I love Aldi grocery stores so much that I started creating Aldi meal plans for them.

We now have many Aldi meal plans to choose from, each meal plan includes at least 20 meals for under $150.

You can access all of those meals plan at *bit.ly/ aldiplans.*

Shopping at Aldi can mean huge savings in a short amount of time. Combine both couponing and shopping at Aldi, and your grocery bill may be cut in half in no time!

68

# 13

## HOW YOUR GROCERY STORE FLYERS CAN HELP YOU SAVE THOUSANDS PER YEAR

**Your weekly store flyer is a gold mine** of information; just by looking at the front page you know what the best deals are. The deals there are called 'Loss Leaders.' This means the store is taking a loss by offering them at deeply discounted prices. They hope that these loss

leaders will lure you into their store to do the rest of your grocery shopping. So how do you use this information to meal plan and save with coupons?

There are a few different ways to use store flyers to your benefit and help you save thousands per year:

1. You can shop only the loss leaders at multiple stores; this will guarantee that you will get the best deals at each store. It does take some time, but if you have time and your stores are relatively close to each other, this may be the option for you.

2. You can price match the loss leaders from multiple stores at one store. Bring your store flyers with you to either Walmart or Target, and they will give you the price listed in other store flyers (this is called price matching). It is easiest to do this at Walmart because you can do it right at the cash register. You simply have to tell them which items you are price matching, BEFORE they ring it up. They will have to adjust the prices down after they scan the items. Target is a little trickier because you have to price match at customer service, so it can take a little bit longer when there is a line.

3. Stock up on the loss leaders every week, and spend the remainder of your money at that store on the rest of your shopping list.

4. Stacking coupons with these loss leaders is usually how I come up with my 'free or cheap list" for the week. You can usually find the best meat sales and the best deals on the front page as these loss leaders.

Now let's talk about product placement in the grocery store and how paying attention to where things are located can save you money too!

# 14

## PAY ATTENTION TO PRODUCT PLACEMENT

**One of the many ways grocery stores** make money is by product placement throughout their stores. You can often find the same items in several spots around the store; ironically, they have different packaging and sometimes VERY different prices.

Take sesame seeds, for example, which Mark and I frequently use for cooking. As you can see, you'd spend $5.49 on this 2.5 oz container of Spice Island sesame seeds. This brand can be found in the spice aisle, where most people look for sesame seeds.

If you travel just two aisles over, you can find a

larger 3.75 oz. container of sesame seeds in the Asian section for only $2.59! You would likely only look for sesame seeds in this aisle if you were making something like sushi, and for every other purpose of sesame seeds, you would go to the  spice aisle and spend $5.49 instead of $2.59.

Another example that I found was on almonds. Most people would probably look for these in the baking aisle first. And there you would find a 5 oz. bag of Diamond almonds for $3.59.

But just the next aisle over you can find an 8 oz. bag for $3.99 (better price per ounce). You can also find these even cheaper in the bulk candy section, which would be closer to the $2.99 price point.

Some other places with marked up items in the grocery store are travel-sized items. You may sometimes pay twice as much for a travel sized item as opposed to an item on sale just a foot away from you.

# CONGRATULATIONS!

You made it to the end of the book! You're ready to start saving some money, right?

Thank you for taking the time to read this book, I know you are busy and your time is precious, so I really appreciate it! I hope you've learned how to make couponing as simple as possible so you can save money and spend more time with your family.

Couponing can be difficult, but as long as you remember my tips, it should be easier to start and stick with it. I encourage you to continue collecting coupons. Always stay neat and organized to get the most out of your time and money. Stay on top of store coupon policies, check yearly for updates and keep a copy for yourself. Set a grocery budget for your family and make sure you stick to it. Plan your meals with your store circular, and keep your coupons nearby for the most possible savings. Always pair a coupon with a sale item to get the lowest price. Trust me—with a little bit of practice, you will get the hang of it, and it actually becomes fun. The rules will be second nature to you and shopping will be a breeze!

Remember to check out *iamthatlady.com* daily for frrugal living articles and coupon matchups. If you are looking for coupons for a certain product be sure to visit the coupon database on the site. [*bit.ly/coupon-database-10*]

I hope you found this book informative and motivational. Once you experience the benefits of proper couponing, you will be hooked! If you have any questions for me, please don't hesitate to ask!

Sincerely,

*Lauren Greutman*

Want to learn how to budget and get out of debt? Check out my other website *MarkandLaurenG.com* where my husband Mark and I walk your though how to set up a budget, get out of debt, and discover how to live with financial independence.

# NOTES

_____

_____

_____

_____

_____

_____

_____

_____

_____

_____

_____

_____

_____

_____

_____

_____

_____

_____

# NOTES

_____

_____

_____

_____

_____

_____

_____

_____

_____

_____

_____

_____

_____

_____

_____

_____

_____

_____

_____

_____

# NOTES

_____

_____

_____

_____

_____

_____

_____

_____

_____

_____

_____

_____

_____

_____

_____

_____

_____

_____

# NOTES

_____

_____

_____

_____

_____

_____

_____

_____

_____

_____

_____

_____

_____

_____

_____

_____

_____

# NOTES

# NOTES

_____

_____

_____

_____

_____

_____

_____

_____

_____

_____

_____

_____

_____

_____

_____

_____

_____

_____

# NOTES

# NOTES

_____

_____

_____

_____

_____

_____

_____

_____

_____

_____

_____

_____

_____

_____

_____

_____

_____

_____

# NOTES

_____

_____

_____

_____

_____

_____

_____

_____

_____

_____

_____

_____

_____

_____

_____

_____

_____

_____

_____

59322733R00062

Made in the USA
Lexington, KY
31 December 2016